Church
Meets
World

VOLUME 4
in the
**Church's
Teachings
for a
Changing
World**
series

WINNIE VARGHESE

Morehouse Publishing
NEW YORK

Copyright © 2016 by Winnie Varghese

All rights reserved. No part of this book may be reproduced, stored in a retrieval system, or transmitted in any form or by any means, electronic or mechanical, including photocopying, recording, or otherwise, without the written permission of the publisher.

Unless otherwise noted, the Scripture quotations contained herein are from the New Revised Standard Version Bible, copyright © 1989 by the Division of Christian Education of the National Council of Churches of Christ in the U.S.A. Used by permission. All rights reserved.

Morehouse Publishing, 19 East 34th Street, New York, NY 10016

Morehouse Publishing is an imprint of Church Publishing Incorporated.
www.churchpublishing.org

Cover art: *Haiti Earthquake Survivor 2 (Woman and Child)* (watercolor) © 2015 by Janita Lo.

Cover design by Laurie Klein Westhafer

Typeset by Beth Oberholtzer

Library of Congress Cataloging-in-Publication Data

Names: Varghese, Winnie, author.
Title: Church meets world / Winnie Varghese.
Description: New York : Morehouse Publishing, 2016. | Series: Church's teachings for a changing world series ; VOLUME 4 | Includes bibliographical references. | Description based on print version record and CIP data provided by publisher; resource not viewed.
Identifiers: LCCN 2016019893 (print) | LCCN 2016016601 (ebook) | ISBN 9780819232724 (ebook) | ISBN 9780819232717 (pbk.)
Subjects: LCSH: Church and the world.
Classification: LCC BR115.W6 (print) | LCC BR115.W6 V37 2016 (ebook) | DDC 261/.1—dc23
LC record available at https://lccn.loc.gov/2016019893

Printed in the United States of America

Contents

Acknowledgments

In college I found a copy of *The Witness* magazine at the Episcopal Chaplaincy at Southern Methodist University and knew The Episcopal Church was for me. My family comes from the Asian Orthodox Christian communities in Kerala in India. Because of the nature of British occupation and the politics of independence, the faith in which I was reared always included the language of devotion, resistance, and justice. Ours was a heritage of heroes like Bishop Paul Varghese (no relation) and M. M. Thomas, men and women that I grew up assuming were the true image of what it meant to be a Christian. I am proud to inherit their convictions around faith, justice, and hope, and I am grateful to share them here.

This book is by no means comprehensive, and many urgent issues are not addressed. I hope my limitations inspire you to fill in the gaps.

Stephanie Spellers is the best pastor editor and has been a patient friend through a year of unexpected changes in my life. What is worthwhile in this book is a testament to her persistence and encouragement.

I am proud to be the daughter of Cherian and Leelamma who taught us to be generous and open-minded Christians in Texas. We try.

Finally, I am grateful to walk through life with Elizabeth, who changes the world for the better daily, but not tirelessly.

Introduction
Why Justice?

About a decade ago, I was on a panel in a suburban church seated next to one of my heroes, a woman who was a first in practically every way in her generation in the church, bold and courageous in ways I only hoped I might be some day.

I spoke about the need for the church to be a leader in movements for social change, because we have been given a vision of a just society in the proclamation of the prophets, in the life and teachings of Jesus, and in the Eucharistic feast. Our faith compels us to deeply desire justice, and equips us to work for it.

My hero leaned in after I sat down and asked, "Do you really believe that?"

I hope we all do.

Why Justice?

The Bible tells us that God cares very much for God's creation, which includes people. The central story of the Hebrew people is their liberation from slavery in Egypt at the command of God. Throughout the Hebrew Scriptures the prophets call the authorities to rule justly, with particular attention to those most vulnerable, the poor, foreigner, widow, and orphan.

In the church from the beginning, we see followers of Jesus trying to create communities that reflect these values of fairness and equity. In the first church communities in the **Acts of the Apostles**, recounted in the first chapters after the Gospels, the disciples gather a community and pool their resources together so that all have enough. The church was intimately involved in the details of how people live in this world, with deacons and bishops working to provide for all and to help in times of crisis.

Christian communities have historically created social institutions involved with the whole person: schools and hospitals as well as churches and monasteries. Often all of these institutions were combined in one mission site.

Justice asks that, along with these acts of mercy and compassion, we work to undo institutions that perpetuate sin, the "principalities and powers" in the letters of Paul that create the conditions of suffering.

The work of reconciliation involves yet another step. **Reconciliation** requires that we work to restore humanity, healing human relationship, but also healing the sacred sense of self lost either by a personal act of violence or by individuals in systems that generate inequality. The perpetrator may have committed a crime, or they may have acted legally in a way that nonetheless degrades another person.

While justice is visualized as a balanced scale, reconciliation is about a return to wholeness and right relation with God and one another, which Paul in 2 Corinthians 5 tells us is possible in Christ.

An Episcopal Approach

What is an Episcopal approach to justice and reconciliation? It includes everything I mentioned above, with some distinct markers:

- Scripture, tradition, and reason in balance. We bring our full selves to the matter at hand both to cast a vision of justice and to work toward it.

- Contextualization. We seek to understand what historical and social forces as well as individual decisions bring us to where we are today.

- Active discernment. We discover where God is at work, or where the work of God is limited by human sinfulness.

Another significant factor in the Anglican approach is our history as an **established church**. We come from the Church of England, which functions as a part of the state. In the English context the church is like a branch of government, and because of that relationship, it tends to the spiritual needs of all of the people in the community regardless of their stated belief or lack of belief. In some ways, we in The Episcopal Church have carried that English and Catholic idea of the **parish**—a geographic area for which a church bears responsibility—through to current times.

In contrast to most Protestants, whose mission extends to those who ascribe to shared beliefs, Anglicans have had and today in England continue to heed a call to tend all the souls in the geographic area known as their parish. The most conservative might believe that means a responsibility to make them all Christians. The most liberal might intend the care of people of whatever belief who live within the parish bounds.

The Episcopal Church is not established in that way, but the legacy of establishment means we can claim as a part of our tradition taking care of a community without regard to their belief or whether they might ever come to church on a Sunday. At our best this translates to a religion that does not stop at the door after worship.

Historically, we have paid attention to the stories of the powerful who become advocates for the powerless. Today, primarily through social media, we hear the voices of the ones who are on the margins of society, claiming their full humanity in the work of justice-making. In this book, and in The Episcopal Church at its best, all of those voices matter—center and margins.

A Twenty-First–Century Approach

In the current century in the United States, it is almost impossible to practice a Christianity that is not heavily influenced by the **Moral Majority** and various fundamentalist forms of Christianity. They are dominant and mainstream in the media and culture, such that one can hardly speak of Christianity without referencing ideas like personal salvation, which would have been anathema to historic Christianity and the traditional understanding of salvation through the church.

This personal emphasis gets counter-balanced with another trend: Around the world, the **post-colonial**, nationalist movements of the late twentieth century fostered a hope for the radical transformation of society in countries once held as colonies of various European powers. Movements in Africa, Asia, and Latin America and the corresponding human rights and civil rights movements in the United States, Canada, the United Kingdom, and Australia were interpreted by the church and theologians of the time as part of the story of God acting in the world on the side of the downtrodden.

As Anglicans we have the privilege of combining these two movements: the personal and the social. We seek a personal transformation or reorientation ("regeneration" is the traditional term) of our lives in light of whom we are made to be in God. We seek self-understanding and revelation, which relates to our place in the society within which we live.

Our approach to social witness is fundamentally pastoral and contextual, which means we begin by engaging the lived reality of real people, including ourselves, working to understand the forces around us that impact human suffering and flourishing. For instance, if you are a Native American living on a reservation, your sense of the space you occupy, the possibilities for your life, your relationship to the country you live in, and your understanding of what is necessary for human flourishing must be influenced by that particular context. The capacity to take in the rich diversity of human experience and respond specifically is a gift of a pastorally focused tradition like ours. We do not tend to seek uniformity among our membership; rather we seek **comprehensiveness**, carefully engaging the many perspectives we all bring.

Taking It to the Streets

It is the work of our salvation to seek justice and serve one another. The work of liturgy, study, prayer, and conversation in our congregations effects a transformation of our personal lives toward an ever-increasing recognition of the humanity of others and the sacredness of creation.

This work for most of us is personally painful. It challenges our assumptions, but more profoundly it pokes at our scars. We are asked to investigate those places in our lives where our compassion is limited by our hurt, and we work toward being the people God has made us to be, free from sin.

This might sound very idealistic to you, and if you disagree, it might sound judgmental. Ultimately, the work of liberation is idealistic and hopeful. It is also concrete and personal. It is tender and teary eyed. It is collegial and movement building. It is brave, and it can be humiliating, which is fitting, as it is a facing into the forces of isolation, contempt, and greed, the same forces the apostle Paul warned about. "For our struggle is not against enemies of blood and flesh, but against the rulers, against the authorities, against the cosmic powers of this present darkness, against the spiritual forces of evil in the heavenly places" (Ephesians 6:12).

According to **William Stringfellow**, an Episcopal theologian, we are confronted with forces of evil in society that are as certain and powerful as death to the individual. But in the resurrection of Jesus Christ, we have a new way. The way of Jesus is the way of liberation, and it must be the work of his church.

That work is often visibly taken up by scholars, political figures, and authors. But I want to acknowledge at the outset that those who do the work of justice in most of our communities are unknown. History may understand the movements to be led by one or two charismatic individuals, but the social pressure that created a platform for a leader is often built by regular people, people like you and me, showing up and working in their own ways for a more just society.

The Episcopal witness in the world is particular to a place and time. We engage the ordinary stuff of life in our worship and take the sacred into our hands. We approach the divine with our own simple language, and we trust that God has made us to bear light in this broken world. In these pages, we will explore just what those common practices and commitments have led us to say and do over time, and how they might inspire us to witness in the days to come.

TO PONDER

1. Imagine two ends of a spectrum: one representing a more personal faith that transforms individual lives and the other end representing a more socially oriented faith that transforms society. To which end do you most naturally gravitate, if any?

2. Name some of the major social movements that have affected your life and the life of your wider community.

3. If you're part of a church, how has your church participated in social movements in that community? What has your church engaged, and what has it not engaged? What did you think of these stands?

4. Paul wrote in Ephesians that "our struggle is not against enemies of blood and flesh, but against the rulers, against the authorities, against the cosmic powers of this present darkness." Does this sound true? How do you respond to his statement?

Chapter 1

Biblical Foundations

He has told you, O mortal, what is good;
and what does the Lord require of you
but to do justice, and to love kindness,
and to walk humbly with your God?
—Micah 6:8

Jim Wallis, a founder of the Sojourner Community in Washington, D.C., tells the story of having an intern cut out every reference to economic justice in a Bible. When Wallis later waved the Bible around during a sermon, it looked moth-eaten. He did the same exercise with another Bible, eliminating references to sexual morality, and the text appeared whole.

The Bible doesn't talk about everything. We don't get a straightforward guide for all of the world's problems, or even for all of our personal worries. However, there is no disputing the fact that the Bible has a lot to say about how we organize our society, how we use our material resources, and how we treat the poor and vulnerable.

Consider the wisdom of Proverbs: "Those who oppress the poor insult their Maker, but those who are kind to the needy honor him" (14:31). Or look to the words of Jesus (read from the scroll of the prophet Isaiah), spoken as he began his public ministry:

> The Spirit of the Lord is upon me,
> because he has anointed me
> to bring good news to the poor.
> He has sent me to proclaim release to the captives
> and recovery of sight to the blind,
> to let the oppressed go free,
> to proclaim the year of the Lord's favor. (Luke 4:18–19)

From the book of Genesis, through the wisdom literature, the prophets, the Gospels, and the stories of the early church, the people of God wrestle with exactly what a just society requires and who is responsible for creating it. They may be conflicted, but when God is speaking, God's values are clear. The God of the people of Israel, the God of Jesus, proclaims justice to the poor and outcast, proclaims the day of the Lord's liberty to the debtor and prisoner, and expects the chosen people to create societies that reflect those values.

Justice in the Hebrew Bible

We know that from the beginning, in creation, all things are created to be in harmony. From the beginning, the striving, shame, and fear of human beings affects the rest of creation, from the Garden of Eden, through the Tower of Babel and the Flood story. The text tells us these human follies only draw God's ire.

Until the **Hebrew people** were enslaved in Egypt, they were less a "people" and more a family, one that had the kinds of problems families have, like jealousy among siblings (Genesis 4 and 50) and favored children (Genesis 16 and 25). It is in enduring slavery together followed by the ordeal of the Exodus from Egypt that the children of Israel forge new bonds that make them a people, the Hebrew people.

They are nomadic for a time, and then they settle in a land called Canaan that had already been settled by others, their distant relations through Noah. For them, it is the Promised Land, literally promised by Yahweh. "I declare that I will bring you up out of the misery of Egypt, to the land of the Canaanites, the Hittites, the Amorites, the Perizzites, the Hivites, and the Jebusites, a land flowing with milk and honey" (Exodus 3:17).

When they settle in this new land, they begin to organize their community as the followers of the God who liberated them from slavery. God has now given them the Law as a guide for establishing their new nation, and among other things it includes strict instructions for how workers, debtors, and outsiders should be treated.

> You shall not withhold the wages of poor and needy laborers, whether other Israelites or aliens who reside in your land in one of your towns. You shall pay them their wages daily before sunset, because they are poor and their livelihood depends on them; otherwise they might cry to the Lord against you, and you would incur guilt. (Deuteronomy 24:14–15)

If they are to be God's people, then they are to live by a certain set of values: acknowledge dependence upon God and practice compassion for the poor, the foreigner, the wanderer, the slave, the widow, and the orphan. The text regularly repeats the litany of the outsiders and disenfranchised, calling Israel to resist what must have been a strong thread of inward-looking, defensive, protective identity that was likely forming in the now-settled nation of Israel.

> If there is among you anyone in need, a member of your community in any of your towns within the land that the Lord your God is giving you, do not be hard-hearted or tight-fisted toward your needy neighbor. You should rather open your hand, willingly lending enough to meet the need, whatever it may be. . . . Give liberally and be ungrudging when you do so, for on this account the Lord your God will bless you in all your work and in all that you undertake. Since there will never cease to be some in need on

the earth, I therefore command you, "Open your hand to the poor
and needy neighbor in your land." (Deuteronomy 15:7–8, 10–11)

Because the Bible begins with the story of a nation, texts like
this about social justice tend to be quite concrete. We may think of
approaching God primarily in prayer and in worship. In the Bible,
God seems less interested in how offerings are made and what
words we use. Instead, justice is named as true worship, as the
Prophet Isaiah reminds the recalcitrant children of Israel:

> Is not this the fast that I choose:
> to loose the bonds of injustice,
> to undo the thongs of the yoke,
> to let the oppressed go free,
> and to break every yoke?
>
> Is it not to share your bread with the hungry,
> and bring the homeless poor into your house;
> when you see the naked, to cover them,
> and not to hide yourself from your own kin? (Isaiah 58:6–7)

This is a challenging passage for Episcopalians. Many would
say worship is our greatest strength; it is also the site at which we
should be most vigilant in watching for betrayal and idolatry. The
forces of sin that create injustice are persistent, and like Israel we
too run the risk of celebrating beautiful yet meaningless worship.

Justice and Jesus

In the gospels we can point to Jesus's teachings on justice, and
they are many. Jesus not only defied the powers of the time in
words; he challenged them in his very being. As a first-century
Jewish peasant living under Roman occupation in Palestine, he
defied local leadership and actively mocked the authority of the
empire. Jesus is placed clearly in the lineage of the children of Israel, and he is born of a barely married young woman, in a family
of modest means, on the outer fringes of the Roman Empire. The

list of Jesus's ancestors in the gospel of Luke features widows, prostitutes, kings, and shepherds.

In other words, he not only stands with oppressed people. He is one of the people, cruelly subjugated by acts of state violence like crucifixion.

What does it mean that God comes among us as one who is powerless and oppressed? Where should we look for God's action in the world? Jesus engages people from all parts of society and from diverse religious backgrounds, and in doing so he locates God's activity in the most unlikely places. He chooses his disciples from among the more modest members of his society and charges them with the all-important message of the reign of God's justice.

Finally, toward the close of his earthly ministry, Jesus offers a parable that appears to sum up the imperative to embrace those who suffer most, not only for their sake but also for our own salvation:

> Then the king will say to those at his right hand, "Come, you that are blessed by my Father, inherit the kingdom prepared for you from the foundation of the world; for I was hungry and you gave me food, I was thirsty and you gave me something to drink, I was a stranger and you welcomed me, I was naked and you gave me clothing, I was sick and you took care of me, I was in prison and you visited me." . . . And the king will answer them, "Truly I tell you, just as you did it to one of the least of these who are members of my family, you did it to me." (Matthew 25:34–36, 40)

We have a God who speaks throughout the Bible on behalf of the oppressed, and in Jesus we have God among us, a Messiah revealed as one of the marginalized.

An Early Church Witness

In the letters of the early church, we see a community that is not just concerned about justice; they are a people without much social influence. The early church lives in opposition to or invisible to larger society.

Within these small communities, we find the values of the Hebrew Scripture emerging again, but on a smaller scale. As James puts it: "Religion that is pure and undefiled before God, the Father, is this: to care for orphans and widows in their distress, and to keep oneself unstained by the world" (James 1:27).

The **Apostle Paul** has a famously mixed record on justice. He commends the leadership of numerous women in Christian communities, like the deacon Phoebe (Romans 16), but then he advises women to cover their heads (1 Corinthians 11:5) and hold their tongues in the community gathering (1 Corinthians 14:33–35). He tells slaves to obey their masters and trust that they will be rewarded on earth and in heaven (Ephesians 6:5–9 and Colossians 3:22). Then he offers a stirring call for equality in Christ in his letter to the Galatians:

> [F]or in Christ Jesus you are all children of God through faith. As many of you as were baptized into Christ have clothed yourselves with Christ. There is no longer Jew or Greek, there is no longer slave or free, there is no longer male and female; for all of you are one in Christ Jesus. (Galatians 3:26–28)

Ultimately, our church teaches that the Scriptures that speak for justice and equality are paramount. Our church does not believe injustice is preordained. Our church does not teach that the way of the world is God's way. We, as followers of Jesus, teach the opposite. We teach that the ways of the world are the ways of the powers and principalities. The ways of God are to be found among the margin dwellers and among the persecuted. They are to be found on the side roads and the edge of town, in the places where it is not safe to go because you might see something that causes you to question the way things are.

A friend from India who was not raised with a religious practice and is from the Dalit community, a group excluded from caste identity in India and targeted for horrible abuse and discrimination, told me about the time he was given a Bible to read in his early twenties. He knew nothing about Christianity, so he read the Bible from the beginning to the end, as you would any other book. By the end he said he was in tears. He had never read a book so clear in its message of freedom and liberation for his community. He asked the friend who gave him the Bible if he could be baptized.

Scripture has the same transformative power for us all, including those who have been in church our whole lives, if we take it at its word.

TO PONDER

1. Do you read the Bible in your personal practice? What role does it play as you make decisions about your life: how you spend money, how you choose your friends, how you understand your sexuality, etc.?

2. What biblical mandates for the social order can you identify? Which ones apply to your life, and which do you think might apply to another community or time?

3. Christians often disagree on what the Bible says about social issues. How do you think we should deal with those differences?

Chapter 2

Church of the Oppressed or the Empire

Why do the teachings of Jesus and the cries for justice in the Hebrew Scriptures seem so antithetical to the kind of church most of us attend each week? Christianity has a complicated relationship with the culture around it.

We were founded as a sect of Judaism, a reform movement among a small group that ultimately became the religion of the Roman Empire. When the Emperor Constantine became a Christian in 312, the church and its members who had defined themselves in opposition to Rome were suddenly insiders. The teachings of the church were interpreted by those who had power, instead of those who were disenfranchised by the empire and for whom the New Testament had been written. It changed everything.

That transition—from Church of the Oppressed to Church of the Empire—is one of the most important in all of Christian history. The teachings of Jesus and the social location of the church in contemporary society, literally where we fit into our society, is something every church must negotiate, and it is fraught for The Episcopal Church.

Allied with Empire?

The Episcopal Church is often identified as a church of the power elite in the United States, and rightly so. After George Washington took the oath of office as the first president of the United States on Wall Street in New York City, he walked down the block to pray at St. Paul's Chapel, today a chapel of Trinity Church Wall Street.

Following the first General Convention of the new Episcopal Church, distinct from the authority of the Church of England, historians have noted that our church entered something like a state of "suspended animation."[1] Clergy were encouraged not to vote on or engage in social or political movements. Our theology pointed over the head of Constantine and back to the early church fathers, who wanted little to do with the state or society.[2] But unlike the early church's disengagement, ours was not for lack of power or because of oppression; it was freely chosen and benefitted the status quo.

We also have a heritage, from both the Evangelical and Anglo-Catholic wings, that has at times prioritized justice for the worker, immigrant, and slave. A small, vocal group has constantly called the church to justice. These histories are in tension, making ours a church of and for the powerful *and* the powerless.

Forced to Take Sides

The issue of **slavery** tore most American denominations apart, but not The Episcopal Church. If there was a significant Episcopal movement for abolition, it was led almost exclusively by African

---

1. Charles C. Tiffany, *A History of the Protestant Episcopal Church in the United States of America* (New York: The Christian Literature Co., 1895), 385.
2. Phyllis Jean Amenda, "God Bless the Revolution: Episcopalians and Social Justice, 1885–1919" (PhD diss., State University of New York-Binghamton), 13.

Americans, sometimes in ecumenical partnership and on rare occasions with the assistance of powerful white allies.

Absalom Jones and **Peter Williams** were the first black men ordained in The Episcopal Church, and both were leaders in the abolition movement. Jones and Williams each established Episcopal congregations in the early 1800s as free black men in the North. Jones founded the African Church of St. Thomas in Philadelphia. Williams founded the African Church of St. Phillip in New York City.

Jones petitioned the U.S. House of Representatives to reverse the Fugitive Slave Act of 1793, the Act which made all black people vulnerable to (re)enslavement. The petition was denied. Meanwhile, Williams cofounded the *Freedman's Journal* and served as a director of the American Anti-Slavery Society.

There were only a few prominent white abolitionists in The Episcopal Church. The best known were the Jay family of New York, and in particular **William Jay**, a founder of the New York City Anti-Slavery Society. Jay was outspoken in opposition to Episcopal bishops who defended slavery, often on biblical grounds. At one point, he found himself in disagreement with the then bishop of New York, John Henry Hobart, who had been Peter Williams's mentor when Hobart was rector of Trinity Wall Street. Bishop Hobart opposed immediate emancipation of slaves and was also an outspoken defender of the uniqueness of The Episcopal Church; he was concerned that the church would be watered down by too high a devotion to the Bible. The emerging Evangelical Movement supported placing a much higher priority on the Bible.

It is worth noting that the **Evangelical Movement** of the time, which Bishop Hobart opposed and Jay supported, called for social justice from a biblical perspective, particularly as it related to slavery and poverty. In the North and the South, The Episcopal Church is notable for its support of slavery among its white members, and leadership in the abolition movement by black members.

For the Common Good

The **Social Gospel Movement** was a movement of the late nineteenth and early twentieth centuries that responded to the new intensity of urban poverty brought on by industrialization in England and the United States. **Walter Rauschenbusch**, a Baptist minister in New York's Hell's Kitchen, in *A Theology for the Social Gospel*, inspired a generation of Christians to work for the "kingdom of God," understood as God's dream for the world, or the perfection of creation in the present.

In the Anglican tradition in England, **Frederick Denison Maurice** was the most influential theologian and clergyman in this area. Like Rauschenbusch, he was convinced that the kingdom of God was not just a future reality but a present, earthly one.

> "The Bible," we are told sometimes, "gives us such a beautiful picture of what we should be." Nonsense! It gives us no picture at all. It reveals to us a fact: it tells us what we really are; it says, This is the form in which God created you, to which He has restored you; this is the work which the Eternal Son, the God of Truth and Love, is continually carrying on within you.[3]

Maurice was a founder of **Christian Socialism**, an influential movement that helped European Socialism to remain closely aligned with Christianity. His writings and activity paralleled the work of Anglo-Catholics who founded and led churches in poor urban areas. From the early to mid-nineteenth century, leaders like **Edward Pusey** took radical stands on the side of the poor. "The cry of the poor reacheth the ear of God," he once preached. "Woe to the man whom the poor shall implead at the Judgment-seat of Christ. Woe to him, for whom they do not plead."[4]

---

3. Frederick Denison Maurice, *The Prayer and The Lord's Prayer: Nineteen Sermons Preached in the Chapel of Lincoln's Inn in the Months of February, March, and April 1848* (Eugene, OR: Wipf and Stock, 2010), 221.

4. John Richard Orens, *Stewart Headlam's Radical Anglicanism: The Mass, the Masses, and the Music Hall* (Chicago: University of Illinois Press, 2003), 6.

Anglo-Catholicism and the Social Gospel didn't penetrate Episcopal life in the same way as it did in England, but the "slum priest"—as the English Anglo-Catholics of the time were called—generated a model still revered in urban Episcopal churches.

Vida Dutton Scudder was among the most influential Episcopalians in bringing the Social Gospel to American shores and challenging the church's bent toward elitism. Born in 1861 in South India into a family that spent four generations in medical missionary service, she was educated in Boston and spent her adult life there. She discovered the Social Gospel in graduate school. About that time, she wrote: "I cannot shut myself away and study medieval legends while today [poverty-stricken] men are perishing for the Bread of Life."[5] This was to become the work of her life. She was a prolific academic and socialist writer, offering challenging words like: "We are all segregated in the prison of class."[6]

Scudder worked to apply the teachings of Jesus to the then new horrors of urbanization and industrialization. She established one of the first settlement houses in the United States, Denison House. At the time, the tenement apartments new immigrants could afford were squalid, and small children worked to help support struggling families. The **Settlement House Movement** encouraged wealthy and middle-class people, overwhelmingly women, to live in community with new immigrants and provide education, health care, and recreation, equipping people in the community to improve their lives.

The Catholic Worker Movement is a product of the same time, and many urban areas still have settlement house programs that originated in this movement. Scudder ultimately concluded that the houses were not nearly enough to address the blight of urban poverty and became a Socialist.

---

5. Vida Dutton Scudder, *My Quest for Reality* (New York: E. P. Dutton, 1952), 93–94.

6. Vida Dutton Scudder, *On Journey* (New York: E. P. Dutton, 1934), 67.

The Legacy of the Social Gospel

Scudder's life maps a critical period in Christian history. We see two fiercely dueling ideas of Christian life. On one side, salvation is seen as a primarily private enterprise concerned with personal relationship with God in anticipation of a radical intervention by God in history that would bring with it God's justice. On the other side was the understanding of salvation as a collective enterprise. This "social" conception of faith expected society itself to reflect the reign of God. This reign of God had to do with personal devotion and holiness, and also had to do with how society was ordered.

Scudder believed at the end of her life that a small prophetic community within the church should call society and the church to justice. The language we have today for the church's responsibility to society comes from this time. The ambivalence we see in the church in claiming its role in public life is also a legacy of this time.

TO PONDER

1. Recall the story of the Emperor Constantine and Christianity's shift from religion of the margins to religion of the insiders. What difference do you imagine this made in the experience of Christians who were alive for both eras?

2. The Episcopal Church did not oppose or split over slavery. What does this demonstrate for you about The Episcopal Church?

3. F. D. Maurice and Vida Scudder were very public Christian Socialists. What does this phrase mean for you, if anything, today?

What Is "Power"?

I work for Trinity Church Wall Street in New York City as the Priest for Justice and Reconciliation. You might note some irony there. Trinity is one of the wealthiest, if not the wealthiest church in the Anglican Communion. Trinity has power. We who work at Trinity have power over how money is spent and what voices are heard.

I come to the idea of power as someone formed by statements like "power does not concede power easily." These words were spoken by abolitionist and former slave Frederick Douglass, who attained a position of significant influence in the halls of power in his own lifetime. I have spent most of my life in the church on the margins, working for the full dignity and human rights of those distanced from power. That's where I always thought I would stand, but like many who work in The Episcopal Church, I am also a steward of resources and power.

The Episcopal Church is an institution that has amassed enormous resources to support the thriving of a small number of people. As an institution we potentially have enormous power to work for social change in our local communities, in our local and national government, and in the Anglican Communion. We have often chosen to exercise that power by supporting the status quo.

Power can be exercised in multiple arenas personally and institutionally. There is the power of a government and its military, police, and courts to work for or against justice. There is also a more intangible power: the power to control cultural assumptions regarding who is good and who is bad, who is smart and who is diminished, who is presumed to be innocent and who is presumed guilty. You see power in the structures that decide who can be murdered with impunity, and whose life is treated as precious.

Power can be shared, as when disparate groups finally sit at the same table. But in the work of justice, power cannot be ignored. Although you and I may sit at a table, talk about things we hold in common, and explore what makes us different, when we walk away from the table and back into the wider society, some of us are more safe, have more opportunity, and exercise fuller citizenship, while others of us are perpetually labeled criminal, suspicious, or overall problematic.

Power can be difficult to talk about, because most of us feel powerless over many things: death, illness, and injustice. In the context of a conversation about justice, acknowledging power does not assume that one feels powerful, or that one is powerful over all things. Power in a social analysis is acknowledging how one is *perceived* in society, and the power or privilege that comes with perceived identity. This is not a comment on intentions. It is a comment on the systems within which we function.

Power is a societal force, like gravity is a physical force. It privileges some, whether they want it or not, and disadvantages others. Race, class, gender, gender identity, sexual orientation, and physical ability are some of the categories within which a social power differential operates. As individuals, we can align ourselves with powerful institutions in how we pursue our education, where we work, or where we worship. All that power comes into play when we talk about justice, faith, and reconciliation.

TO PONDER

1. Racism is defined as discrimination plus power: in other words, your personal bias, plus the capacity to impact another person's life negatively because of that bias. Can you think of examples of how this formula works, for racism and other kinds of oppression?

2. In what categories do you have power or privilege? How does that feel? How did you become aware of it?

3. Identify things you can do with your power to challenge injustice.

Chapter 3

Contemporary Voices for Justice

The existential crisis of the Western Christian church in the twentieth century is the **Holocaust**. Christian people in Christian nations organized and participated in an attempted genocide of Jewish people who had been their friends and neighbors.

It was not the first time one group rained terror down on another. Colonialism brought death on a comparable scale to Asia, Africa, and Latin America: Belgium in the Congo, the British in Africa and India, the Spanish in Central and South America. The American story begins with an attempted genocide of the native peoples.

Colonial history, as understood by the Christian church, claimed that a civilized people conquered and thus "saved" a less civilized, non-Christian people, at the same time delivering land into colonial hands. Newspapers of the times include stories of atrocities in faraway colonies, but as horrible as these acts were, they were generally accepted in the teaching of the church. Likewise, while radical political movements of the time protested some of these developments, little happened to question the fundamental good of the Western Man and the Western Imperial Project.

The Holocaust was different. The barbarism of the Holocaust was within the geographic boundaries of the West and was conducted upon people whose humanity was, frankly, less contested than that of the conquered peoples of the far reaches of empire. Archbishop William Temple in England, horrified by the Holocaust, defended participation in World War II as a righteous response to evil.

Theology in a Broken World

One of the horrors of the Holocaust is that too many Christians said nothing at all, and in Europe they even colluded with the German state. Eventually, a few dissenting German Christians like **Dietrich Bonhoeffer** and **Martin Niemoller** emerged, best known because of their relationships with English and American seminaries.

These leaders faced a stark theological crisis: modernity, science, technology, and progress had not made society more good, tolerant, and kind, but instead made evil and tyranny more efficient. In their anguish, they birthed a Protestant theology that featured a demanding personal and communal piety coupled with an organized resistance to political injustice.

After the war, in the United States, soldiers returned home with radically changed consciousness. In particular, Asian, Latino, Native American, and black men who had fought for the freedom of Europe alongside white counterparts now returned to a nation in which they were second-class citizens. The seeds were planted for a radical change in how American Christians understood their personal responsibility to work for the political realization of their God-given dignity and freedom in Christ.

The **liberal and neo-orthodox theologies** that described a benevolent God in a benevolent and progressing world had failed. Some declared God dead. Others turned to the Bible to seek the voice of God for their time.

Voices of Liberation

William Stringfellow may have been the most important Episcopal voice in this moment. Swiss theologian Karl Barth once famously called him the most important American theologian alive.

Stringfellow was a white man, a lawyer and lay theologian, who lived among and defended poor people of color in Harlem. Beginning in the late 1950s and early 1960s through the 1980s, Stringfellow developed what was at the time an utterly unique approach to biblical theology. In fact, many understand his method to be a precursor to **liberation theology**, the theological approach that boldly claims a gospel of freedom for and with those on the underside of society.

At a time when other Christian theologians were resisting an overemphasis on sin, Stringfellow carefully pointed to the overwhelming nature of social sin, injustice, war, and discrimination, all of which smothered life.

> The biblical lifestyle is always a witness of resistance to the status quo in politics, economics, and all society. It is a witness of resurrection from death. Paradoxically, those who embark on the biblical witness constantly risk death—through execution, exile, imprisonment, persecution, defamation, or harassment—at the behest of the rulers of this age. Yet those who do not resist the rulers of the present darkness are consigned to a moral death, the death of their humanness. That, of all the ways of dying, is the most ignominious.[1]

Laywoman **Verna Dozier** sounded many of the same themes not long after Stringfellow. Dozier was an African-American educator and church leader from Washington, D.C. In her seminal text, *The Dream of God*, she announced: "I believe the Christian

---

1. William Stringfellow, *Instead of Death* (New York: Seabury Press, 1976), 100, 101.

church has distorted the call, narrowed it from a call to transform the world to a call to save the souls of individuals who hear and heed a specific message, narrowed it from a present possibility to a future fulfillment."[2]

Following in Stringfellow's and Dozier's footsteps, **Carter Heyward** was one of the Philadelphia 11, the first women ordained in The Episcopal Church. She is also one of the most influential Episcopal theologians of the late twentieth century, emphasizing the idea of God incarnate as verb or "Godding," that is, God at work in acts of mutuality in relationship. This idea infuses most of contemporary Episcopal thought. God, the source of our being, our grounding, is alive and at work when we choose to act in ways that are vulnerable, honest, mutual, and loving. She insists these acts have the power to resist the most profound and violent evil, as we see in the life of Jesus.[3]

Heyward, Dozier, and Stringfellow remind the church that our calling is to live this life fully and to love one another well enough to secure equality and justice for all. Stringfellow brings the Bible to bear on every system, institution, or idea that denies life and dignity. Dozier calls us to a spirituality that is in this world and that is eucharistic, biblical, and urgent. Heyward locates the potential for God to be active in the world in the bodies of Christians who choose right relation.

Faith and Liberation outside the Episcopal Lens

Throughout the second half of the twentieth century and into the twenty-first century, liberation theologies flourished in the United States and beyond. **James Cone**, the father of black liberation theology, placed the lives of black people in the United States at the

---

2. Verna Dozier, *The Dream of God* (New York: Church Publishing, 2006), 5.

3. Carter Heyward, *Touching Our Strength: The Erotic as Power and the Love of God* (San Francisco: Harper & Row, 1989), 188.

center of the biblical narrative. He wondered out loud what the Gospels could mean, if the story of Jesus is for black people too.

As Episcopalians we look to American examples like these, but also to the great teachers and preachers of the Anglican Communion.

Mandathilparampil Mammen (M. M.) Thomas was a Mar Thoma lay leader in the Ecumenical Movement who drew various parts of the Christian family beyond divisions and toward mutual cooperation. The Mar Thoma Church, a Reformed Orthodox Church in India, is in communion with The Episcopal Church and the Anglican Communion.

M. M. Thomas interpreted the Christian doctrine of "Salvation" as "**Humanization**." By Humanization he meant a change for the vast majority of the world's population who live in subhuman conditions. He argued that endemic poverty, famine, cycles of war, and displacement are examples of making the human experience less than human. In that context, salvation, rather than removing us from our humanity, brings us more deeply into a human experience with the dignity and honor that a being in the image of God deserves.

Contextual theologies of the developing world and new nation states of the late twentieth century greatly influenced The Episcopal Church. Onto this stage walked **Desmond Tutu**, Archbishop Emeritus of Cape Town, an almost mythic character in the Anglican Communion.

Tutu once famously said: "If you are neutral in situations of injustice, you have chosen the side of the oppressor. If an elephant has its foot on the tail of a mouse, and you say that you are neutral, the mouse will not appreciate your neutrality."[4]

During the 1970s he, like many South Africans, was working to end apartheid. In the 1980s, as the movement began to make

---

4. Robert McAfee Brown, *Unexpected News: Reading the Bible with Third World Eyes* (Philadelphia: Westminster Press, 1984), 19.

progress and gather international support, he became the first black archbishop of Cape Town, a significant accomplishment on its own and a fraught position. Student marches often started in front of his cathedral, St. George's in Cape Town.

He was awarded the Nobel Peace Prize in 1984 when he was still throwing on his cassock to stand between young people and the police in clashes in front of the cathedral. He is remembered by many of this generation as the convener of the **Truth and Reconciliation Commission**. In postapartheid South Africa, the Commission organized hearings to hear the true stories and often harrowing confessions of brutality under apartheid, and thus to pave the way toward forgiveness and healing.

Tutu is known for his clear-eyed yet openhearted approach to forgiveness and reconciliation. "Forgiving is not forgetting," he wrote in *The Book of Forgiving: The Fourfold Path for Healing Ourselves and Our World*, "it's actually remembering—remembering and not using your right to hit back. It is a second chance for a new beginning. And the remembering part is particularly important. Especially if you don't want to repeat what happened."[5]

Archbishop Tutu has continued to be an outspoken advocate for the dignity of all persons, and he inspires people everywhere to knit a profound personal faith in Jesus Christ together with transformative and redemptive social action.

Liberation Returns to the Mainstream

The liberationist perspective has come in and out of favor in the church's life, especially at the turn of the twenty-first century. Many balk at the challenge it presents to the comfortable of the world, people like me and many of you who are reading this book.

---

5. Desmond Tutu and Mpho Tutu, *The Book of Forgiving: The Fourfold Path for Healing Ourselves and Our World* (San Francisco: Harper One, 2014), 37.

Long associated with Communists and insurgent political movements in Latin America and with the radical politics of the 1960s, **liberationists** have stood on the side of the outcast and despised and announced that God's justice means justice for them.

The election of **Pope Francis** in 2013 brought liberation theology back into the Christian mainstream. He calls for a "poor church for the poor" re-centering the work of the Catholic Church with the outcast.

Michael Curry, elected the twenty-seventh presiding bishop of The Episcopal Church in 2015, carries on the tradition of a liberationist approach. He is known for engaging the Bible with an intellectual acumen and theological and spiritual seriousness that guides us toward personal holiness *and* social justice. His message of love, liberation, and discipleship calls us to action.

> Jesus didn't start an institution, he started a movement. The same movement as Abraham and Sarah. The same movement as Moses and the Israelites. The same movement Amos described, when he said, "Let justice roll down like a river, and righteousness like an ever flowing stream." This is a movement commissioned and commanded by God to transform this world from the nightmare we've too often made it, and into the dream that God has intended all along.[6]

• • •

The theological response to the evil humans can do to one another is to stand on the side of the suffering. Liberation movements look for the action of God there among the powerless. The Episcopal Church constantly struggles to be faithful, in the midst of what can feel very much like a world on the brink.

---

6. Michael Bruce Curry (Reflection offered to Episcopal-Lutheran Clergy Conference at Chico Hot Springs Conference Center, March 29, 2016).

GOING DEEPER

1. Many say the Holocaust was unique in Western history. Is this true? How would such an event challenge one's faith in God today?

2. M. M. Thomas writes that "humanization" for the most downtrodden among us was the work of the Incarnation. Is this true? How does God coming among us change your understanding of the human and of the divine?

3. Liberation movements assume God is especially active among the powerless. What do you think? Have you felt God active in your own life, when you were in great need?

Chapter 4

For the Love of the Earth

Sacred writings are bound in two volumes,
that of creation and that of Holy Scripture.
—*Thomas Aquinas*

In the stories of nearly all people of faith, place is sacred. Creation, both the cosmos and the relationship of God with it, is the beginning of our collective story as Christians. The stewardship of the earth is the first work of the human creature, arguably the mission given by God to humanity. The natural world is the design of the Creator and infused with the Word, made flesh in Jesus.

There are more than a thousand references to the earth in the Bible. Creation begins with the creation of a garden. Revelation ends with a tree by a river, as the source of healing for the city. The declaration of **jubilee** among the Hebrew people, a Sabbath for all, includes a year of rest for the land. Jesus walks through the countryside and encounters God in the wilderness, high places, and finally in a garden. It is in proper relationship to the natural world that humans are in proper relationship to God.

This Fragile Earth

Archbishop of Canterbury **William Temple** in the Gifford Lectures in 1934 described creation as a "Sacramental Universe," meaning the grace of God is at work in the created order as well as through the sacraments of the church. God acts and reveals God's self in creation.

Episcopalians are led to see the face of God in creation and care deeply about the environment through our liturgy. The 1979 Book of Common Prayer is replete with prayers that celebrate the sacredness of creation and the human responsibility to steward it as a gift from God.

At the opening of Eucharistic Prayer C, we offer thanksgiving to God for this gift: "At your command all things came to be: the vast expanse of interstellar space, galaxies, suns, the planets in their courses, and this fragile earth, our island home." These prayers were written in that time when we were seeing the first pictures of the earth from space, like a delicate blue green marble afloat in a mysterious sea. Today we know more about that interconnectedness than ever before.

In more recent years, what had been known poetically about interconnectedness and theologically about the earth as the body of God has become lived reality. We watch the evidence and consequences of climate change mounting before our eyes: rising temperatures, super storms, desertification, and melting snowcaps. The plight of animals and humans vulnerable to climate change has awakened the church to the limits of an **extractive economy** (removing things from the earth like oil and coal). As people of faith, we must consider factors other than short-term benefits, efficiency, or corporate ambition if we are to have a healthy environment now and in generations to come.

We can see what had been predicted: the impact on the environment of industrial farming and the enormous quantities of waste it introduces into the water supply, and the horrifying conditions animals must survive to become our food, which makes them and us sick. The irony that we have taken the gifts of creation given for our care and nourishment and turned them into sites of disease and destruction is perverse if not sinful.

Through science, we have learned in the twenty-first century the depth of our interconnectedness. The seemingly inevitable drive of progress that mowed down forests and turned over prairies is slowly being turned around, as we learn that the earth and climate are intimately connected to one another. The ways of nature are ultimately necessary, ultimately victorious, and not for us to manipulate.

Voices for the Earth

Perhaps one of the most important foundational figures in this work is **Matthew Fox**, the Episcopal priest who coined the term **"Creation Spirituality."** He describes it this way:

> As a movement, Creation Spirituality becomes an amazing gathering place, a kind of watering hole for a person whose passion has been touched by the issues of our day—deep ecologists, ecumenists, artists, native peoples, justice activists, feminists, male liberationists, gay and lesbian peoples, animal liberationists, scientists seeking to reconnect science and wisdom, people of prophetic faith traditions—all these find in the Creation Spirituality movement a common language and a common ground on which to stand.[1]

Creation Spirituality finds its sources in the Wisdom Tradition in the Bible and is committed to an understanding of **immanence** (God's presence at the heart of all things) as well as **transcendence** (God above all things) as critical to a complete understanding of the nature of creation and our relationship within it.

---

1. Matthew Fox, *Creation Spirituality: Liberating Gifts for the People of the Earth* (San Francisco: HarperSanFrancisco, 1991), 16–17.

Global and Local Action

What began as an awareness of the emerging ecological crisis and simple efforts to reconnect with the cycles of the earth locally expresses itself today in social and political action through the Anglican Communion, in The Episcopal Church, and in a variety of local movements.

Anglicans for the Environment

The **Anglican Communion Environment Network** brings together representatives from around the communion, often facing similar challenges and connected by global climate changes.

- Bishops in dioceses threatened by rising sea levels
- Churches with old inefficient buildings
- Farmers losing land
- Communities losing their land to deforestation and desertification
- Congregations that want to consume ethically produced products
- Activists for sustainable environmental practices

The **Episcopal Ecological Network** (EpEN) does much of the same work at a church-wide level. This grassroots network drives energy toward protecting the environment and preserving creation. Their website features lots of resources for reflection, action and worship: www.eenonline.org.

General Convention

The General Convention has passed many resolutions asking the church to study the impact of climate change, genetically modified crops, and the impact of certain industries on vulnerable populations, specifically on the urban and rural poor and people living on reservations. These resolutions emerge from communities directly impacted and root our policies in the lived realities of our fellow Episcopalians.

In 2015 the Convention passed legislation requiring certain church-wide funds "to divest from fossil fuel companies and reinvest in clean renewable energy in a fiscally responsible manner."

Farm and Garden Ministries

The twenty-first century has seen a rise in farm and garden ministries, through our monastic communities, churches, the young adult intentional communities of the Episcopal Service Corps, and school ministries. Churchyard gardens are being used to grow food, often in raised beds when the soil is toxic. Parishes are supplying food pantries with produce from their own gardens. Sunday School curricula on the earth have children in churchyards planting, tending, and harvesting. Groups passionate for this work are coming together in unprecedented ways, especially via the **Episcopal Faith, Food and Farm Network** (www.faith foodfarm.org).

The trend is paralleled in the culture at large. What had been considered inefficient, primitive, farming practices are returning as sustainable methods for safe and nutritious food with local control. The local artisanal food movement in wealthy countries is paralleling movements for control of the resources required to farm in poor countries.

We are seeing a reconnection to the cycles of the earth in our teaching and our living that has brought back practices forgotten by urban and suburban Christians like **Rogation Days** (periods to pray for the harvest and for the labor of our hands) and the blessing of the fields.

Return to the Labyrinth

The **labyrinth** movement, particularly outdoor labyrinths drawn to recall the ancient maze-like paths in cathedrals like Chartres in France, has become a symbol of our renewed commitment to the care of the earth. Labyrinths are often found inside church buildings, but they can also be outside and made with fine or scavenged materials. In their very preparation they have become a way for congregations to reconnect with the grounds of their church. The practice of labyrinth walking combines attentiveness and prayer with attention to the God at work within us and in the natural world.

The Rev. Dr. Lauren Artress is an advocate for the labyrinth as a tool for spiritual renewal. "Labyrinths are powerful blueprints that order chaos, offer a path of prayer, heal deep wounds, serve as a place of solace, and transform human consciousness individually and in community. The labyrinth offers a spiritual exercise that becomes the path of life. It allows the wandering soul to find a way to center, to find a way home."[2]

Our disconnection from the natural world is a disconnection from God the Creator, and it can manifest as un-rooted-ness in our own purpose in the world. In urban environments labyrinths and churchyard gardens can be tools of that sacred reconnection.

A Season of Creation

The movement to observe a liturgical season of creation began in the 1990s. Creation is a series of four weeks that can be used in any time in the year, but usually begin in early September and conclude with **St. Francis's Day** on the first Sunday in October. As a church, we have traditionally provided resources to honor our interconnectedness to the earth. The season of creation emphasizes passages in the Bible that teach of the sacredness of the cycles of the earth with prayers and music that highlight the beauty and complexity of God's creation.

Through most of the liturgical year we reflect upon God's relationship to human beings. In this season we recall God's relationship to all creation.

---

2. Lauren Artress, *Walking a Sacred Path: Rediscovering the Labyrinth as a Spiritual Practice* (New York: Penguin Publishing), 194.

Episcopal Buildings

The elephant in the room in a conversation about environmentalism is our stewardship of our own inherited resources. Church buildings are beloved to our members but notoriously inefficient for the environment. Often these buildings are now home to congregations much smaller than the buildings were built to accommodate.

Some of these buildings are open once or twice a week, or funded by rental to often worthy programs to offset the utilities and maintenance costs. They are expensive and wasteful to heat or cool, if that is even possible given the design and scale of the buildings. One must ask, is this the worship that God requires of us?

Energy surveys are both a way to reduce costs and to live more gently on the earth. With more information, we can improve energy efficiency, harvest water, and use smarter technologies for heating and cooling, so that our buildings and grounds reflect our care for the earth. We must align our physical plants, buildings, and grounds, with our theology. They are the most visible signs of what we believe, and the places where the church concretely meets the world.

TO PONDER

1. What signs of climate change have you noticed in your community? What do you understand the causes to be?

2. How do you engage the created order? In what ways do you sense God in creation?

3. What does "stewardship of the earth" mean to you? Do you see your faith community tending to the earth in concrete ways? What more could you do?

Interlude

What Is "Social Location"?

A friend from seminary taught a class on the New Testament at Sing Sing, the maximum-security prison for men in New York State. He said the men offered the most insightful reflection on Paul's writings that he had ever heard. First he was surprised, but then he says he realized, of course, they're in prison; Paul was in prison. Their social location made all the difference in what they saw in the text.

Social location is a lens or a way of seeing, one that notices all the parts of a person's identity—national origin, class, race, gender expression, and other factors—and invites introspection and honesty. These factors influence how we understand the world around us, our perspectives, our biases, and our gifts.

In biblical studies social location is used as a tool for understanding the world in which the authors of the Bible lived, including who the authors were, who their audiences were, and what the author was trying to accomplish. This kind of analysis can be done by comparison with other texts from the same time period and through archaeological work from which we understand ancient societies. When we do not put ancient texts into their appropriate contexts, we risk assuming biblical writers were directly addressing our current context—our technology, science, identity, and citizenship. We also risk missing out on important connections those writers were making with their audience.

In sociology, in anti-oppression trainings, or in any setting where we're listening across perceived differences, social location is a tool to locate ourselves concretely in time and place.

This kind of identification can seem counter-productive to Christian community. Instead of naming only our similarities as children of God, we notice and name particularities. Why? Social location is one way to honor the diversity present in any group. It challenges the idea that any of us could be objective or solely rational in our thinking. Everyone is shaped by the social categories we live within, whether we accept or resist them.

Social location can also be a powerful tool to confront shame. Whether people feel shame because of family of origin, gender, class or wealth, race, or immigration status, recognizing social location makes the facts of our lives merely that—facts—and not moral shackles fraught with the societal judgment.

Social location can help us to see what is not easily visible in a group and can add to the richness of a conversation, revealing more of the diversity of perspectives we need around the table.

QUESTIONS

1. What is your social location: gender, race, class, age? What else would you include?

2. What does it feel like to state your social location?

3. In what way does this exercise make you feel empowered? In what way is it challenging? Why might that be?

Chapter 5

Racism Matters

In 2012 in Florida, a young man named **George Zimmerman**, acting as a volunteer neighborhood watchman, shot to death **Trayvon Martin**, a black teenager. Martin was walking home from the store with a bag of Skittles in his hand, listening to music through headphones. Zimmerman reported that he saw someone he knew was up to no good, stopped him, attacked him, and killed him. In the course of the event, Zimmerman called the local police who ordered him to avoid a direct confrontation.

In Florida, "**Stand Your Ground**" laws mean that you have the right to shoot someone if you feel threatened. George Zimmerman was acquitted in Trayvon Martin's shooting death because he said that he was scared by the existence of a black teenager walking in his neighborhood.

In 2014 Officer **Darren Wilson** in Ferguson, Missouri, shot **Michael Brown** to death. Michael Brown, like Trayvon Martin, was walking; Darren Wilson, like George Zimmerman, was in a car and armed. Wilson shot Brown to death midday in a busy neighborhood, and Brown's dead body was left on the road for four hours while the neighborhood gathered and watched. Wilson also argued that he felt threatened, and he too was acquitted.

Protests, led by young people of color, followed and sparked a new movement for equal justice under the law, marked by the hashtag #blacklivesmatter. For many in the movement and many who watch from the sidelines, the deaths and the jury acquittals are a reminder of how racism is built into the law and the basic functioning of American life.

Racism Defined

So, what is racism?

Most simply racism sounds like it would be discriminating against a person because of their race. Some would say that **discrimination** is a personal slight or preference, but **racism** is defined as when the person discriminating has the power to cause real harm to another because of their race.

If that is the case, where does that power come from? Why are some people by virtue of their race more powerful than others? Why are some people because of their race presumed to be innocent and some guilty?

Some historians describe slavery and the genocide of Native Americans as the founding sins of the United States. Describing it in this way assumes that a nation or a group of people can sin, not just an individual. There is no avoiding the fact that The Episcopal Church was founded in a nation based on a complex mix of immigrants from Europe who established much of their wealth by the enslavement of African people and the conquering and forced resettlement of Native peoples.

This is a part of American history that we struggle to tell honestly. Why talk about that now? Most Christians understand their faith as one that receives God's forgiveness and love and returns that forgiveness and love to others in response to our awareness of God's love for us.

If that is the nature of faith, then why is it that white Christian men and women lynched men and women who were not white through the twentieth century? Why would Christian women and men drive people off their lands and leave them to die? How could Christian women and men abuse and destroy the bodies and spirits of people they believed they owned? How can some of us say almost every moment of our lives is defined by race, and others say they do not see race or color? What do we mean when we say some people have "privilege" and others cannot be racist?

Like other issues addressed in this book, your experience might be that these issues are pressing for you. They weigh on your heart and mind, and you long to know how to follow Jesus in this path. For others, this might seem like dredging up old history to explain misunderstandings today.

The ways of God mean that like the new church in Acts, we tell our stories over and over again, telling the truth, and drawing out the liberating thread, those brave souls who modeled what is right, to guide us to freedom. That brings us back to a deeper engagement around race and ethnicity.

#BlackLivesMatter

As I write this, **#blacklivesmatter** is a young and flourishing movement. The hashtag, the web presence, and the structure of the movement are the brainchild of three queer women of color: **Patrice Cullors**, **Alicia Garza**, and **Opal Tometi**. It is evidenced in protests and in information sharing, and it is creating a movement to change the way policing happens and the way race is construed in the United States.

Patterns of racial hostility from private citizens and from police toward African Americans have long been known and discussed, particularly within communities of color and among police officers. What is different today is that social media has created a platform to document the regular incidence of the killing of black people by the police. The hashtag created the capacity for anyone to document an action, a concern, or reflection or to share news through their networks.

Public awareness of the origins of policing as slave patrols and the legacy of that history has been exposed in an entirely new way.

- **Mass incarceration**, disproportionately affecting black, Hispanic and Native American men, has emerged from draconian drug laws and the for-profit prison system, which are proving to be both unsustainable and indefensible.

- The militarization of our police force during the drug war and the use of excess military supplies and personnel from two land wars has led to policing that is more like a military occupation, in which you are holding a territory against an enemy, than a public safety officer watching out for the well-being of the entire community.

- In our public schools, police act as security officers, arresting children as young as elementary school and taking them to holding cells for infractions that are the regular behaviors of children.

Policing in the United States is coming under scrutiny in the same way that access to equal education and the vote did in the Civil Rights Movement in the middle of the last century. In that moment, the church stepped up in profound ways.

In response to the Civil Rights Act of 1965 and ongoing protests and riots, Presiding Bishop John Hines in 1967 called for the **General Convention Special Program** to engage and empower racial minorities. The next presiding bishop, Edmund Browning, continued the work of racial justice, but as the church and its budgets have grown smaller, and the debates over human sexuality have become communion-wide struggles, the work to eradicate racism has become less prominent in our work as a church.

That shifted in 2015. The General Convention occurred in the shadow of the massacre of black members of Mother Emmanuel African Methodist Episcopal Church in Charleston,

South Carolina. In a way that is unprecedented since the 1960s, the church's leaders committed millions of dollars and significant church energy to strategic efforts to dismantle racism in the systems of our church, in the society around us, and in our own hearts.

Beyond Black and White

The most recent commitments to address racism have attempted to link with the voices and experiences of varied communities of color, understanding that the work for racial justice must embrace more than the black and white paradigm that has so marked racial awareness in the United States.

Native Americans and Indigenous Peoples

Native Americans are more likely to be victims of violent crimes perpetrated by non-Native people than any other group. Native American youth make up 1 percent of the youth population, but represent 70 percent of the youth admitted to the Federal Bureau of Prisons.

Why is this the case? One reason is that Native American life has been devalued and criminalized. It began with the **Doctrine of Discovery**, set out in a series of Papal Bulls and European royal pronouncements beginning in the fifteenth century, the Age of Discovery. The doctrine declares that Christian nations have the right to "discover" and lay claim to non-Christian lands. The people "discovered" on these lands could be converted, killed, or enslaved. This doctrine has been used by the United States in the Supreme Court to defend the conquest of North America.

In 2009, The Episcopal Church through its General Convention repudiated and rejected the Doctrine of Discovery, asking the church to investigate its own history and work for the sovereignty and dignity of native peoples. The conquest, murder, and displacement of the native peoples of North America, in some areas in our lifetime, are among the great sins of the founding of the United States. The church's complicity in that history is one of our great sins. How we work for justice and reconciliation in light of the current day legacies of that history is work we must discern urgently.

Native American communities are diverse in many ways: by tribe, geography, urban, rural, income, and educational opportunities. The Episcopal Church is present in Native communities around the country: Alaska, South Dakota, Minnesota, Montana, Los Angeles, Alabama, Oklahoma, Navajoland, and others. In ministry we work to realize the autonomy that we speak to in repudiating the Doctrine of Discovery.

Asian and Asian Americans

The long history of Asians in the United States is poorly understood. The first significant wave of immigrants from Asia were the Chinese who arrived in 1850. From 1907 to 1952 the **Anti-Asian Exclusion Act** essentially stopped immigration from Asia (by 1952 only 100 Indians and 100 Filipinos were permitted to immigrate annually). The **1965 Immigration and Nationality Act** broke ground by significantly increasing the number of Asians allowed to immigrate based upon skill and family connections. By the middle of the twenty-first century, it is projected that Asian Americans will be the largest immigrant group in the United States.

Asian-American identities are diverse and complex. Racism toward Asian Americans is most visible in some version of the **model minority myth** that pictures all Asians as successful over achievers, which erases the reality of poor and working-class Asian Americans. Asian Americans can also be the "perpetual outsiders," suspicious in times of war or national threat.

Since the **September 11 attacks** on the United States, South and West Asian Americans have become targets of racially targeted harassment and violence, because they are perceived to be terrorists or perceived to be Muslim. And in the 2016 presidential election cycle, those who are in fact Muslim have been demonized and even threatened with deportation.

The Episcopal Church has vibrant Asian and Asian American ministries. **Province 8** of The Episcopal Church includes the Dioceses of Taiwan and Micronesia. Asian immigrant congregations flourish throughout the country, and second-, third-, fourth-, and fifth-generation Asian Americans minister in all levels of The Episcopal Church.

Latino and Hispanic Peoples

Latino communities in the United States are diverse in national, racial, and ethnic origin. In The Episcopal Church, **Province 9** includes the dioceses of Colombia, Dominican Republic, Central Ecuador, Littoral Ecuador, Honduras, Puerto Rico, and Venezuela.

In the United States, Spanish speakers as a whole are becoming a significant force in public life, and the diversity of the communities from which people come and with which they identify creates a complexity similar to that of Asian Americans.

The most visible social justice issue that impacts Latinos is **immigration**. In the early twenty-first century, waves of women and children and unaccompanied children appeared in higher numbers at the United States–Mexico border. Immigration from Mexico has been a longstanding political issue, since the United States annexed much of northern Mexico at the conclusion of the Mexican-American War in 1847. In some regions of the country it is said, "We did not cross the border. The border crossed us."

Migration across the border in both directions has persisted since the war, at times becoming politically volatile. The drug war and the border wall have introduced a heightened criminal component, and today the most recent waves of immigrants from Mexico are overwhelmingly refugees from political violence in Central America or economic refugees, often from crises generated from American political intervention.

The Episcopal Church, in its dioceses on the border with Mexico, has poured great energy into justice and safety. Throughout the church, you will find Spanish language congregations, and many second, third, fourth, and older generations of Episcopalians of Hispanic heritage. Recognizing the opportunity to connect in new ways with this fast-growing and evolving community, The Episcopal Church in 2015 invested significantly in Latino new church plants and in resources and leadership development.

• • •

In 2015 The Episcopal Church also made a major move: in electing Michael Bruce Curry as Presiding Bishop, we chose our first African-American primate. The power of the election in this time is hard to overstate. We struggle to talk about race, privilege, and power, and we do not struggle enough to connect the message of freedom in the gospels to all people in their particularity in this time.

The work of dismantling racism is ongoing for us, and the goal is to be a church reflective of whom God intends us to be, and that might not be a church that makes us comfortable. Among bishops and among our clergy and lay leaders, we have decided racial justice and evangelism will be our priority work for the next nine years. It is the work of the healing of the United States and the nations where we are present, the healing of our church, and the healing of our souls.

TO PONDER

1. The Episcopal Church, like many of the mainline denominations, is sometimes called a "White Church." What does that mean to you? Is it true? If so, how can or should we change?

2. Movements for racial justice have occurred throughout history. What do you think the church's role should be in relation to these movements?

3. How are you engaging the work of racial reconciliation? What do you want to learn? Who do you want to work alongside?

Chapter 6

Christian Love

Love is a primary concern for the church. As Christians we say God is love. We do not say that God is like love, or that love is one aspect of God. God, we say, is love.

As human beings we know love in human relationship: the love of and for parents, children, siblings, other family, friends. In particular, Christians place a high value on love that is mutual and expressed physically with security and stability in relationship with a chosen partner.

For these reasons and more, churches tend to engage the larger cultural conversation about human sexuality and marriage with great vigor. In The Episcopal Church, as in so many churches, that struggle comes to a head around questions of inclusion for lesbians, gay men, and transgender and bisexual people, especially who can be ordained and to whom one can be married.

First Strides toward Inclusion

In 1976 the General Convention of The Episcopal Church declared "homosexual persons are children of God who have a full and equal claim with all other persons upon the love, acceptance, and pastoral concern and care of the Church."

It was only in 1973 that the American Psychological Association removed homosexuality from the diagnostic manual of disorders. That shift occurred in the wake of the **Stonewall Riot of 1969**, the public act that launched the gay liberation movement, led by transgender and queer people of color in Manhattan.

In The Episcopal Church we have always had lay and ordained members in same-sex relationships, but the public profession of those relationships, and the understanding of them as honorable and equivalent to relationships between two people of the opposite sex, was a true innovation.

The bulk of the work toward the full inclusion of gay and lesbian persons in The Episcopal Church—including the passage of the landmark resolution in 1976—was led by **Integrity**, an organization founded by **Louie Clay** (née Crew) in 1974. Their work created the conditions for the Rt. Rev. Paul Moore, bishop of New York, to ordain **Ellen Barrett**, the first out gay priest in 1977.

The nature of the movement for the full inclusion of gay people in the life of the church changed in the 1980s and 1990s because of the **HIV/AIDS pandemic**. When HIV/AIDS was first emerging, young gay men were becoming sick and dying quickly and horribly, but homophobia prevented the funding of appropriate public health practices. The resulting activism to demand research and access to better treatment politicized the nation.

The motto of the time was "silence = death." Celebrities and ordinary people "came out"—many at first because they were dying, but as time went on, because it was a matter of integrity or honesty. In the church, people who were known and beloved were now sick: friends, brothers, sons, musicians, priests, and vestry members. Priests came out in pulpits, and congregations and bishops had decisions to make about people they had known for a long time.

This was an extremely painful time for many, and lots of vocations to church leadership were lost. The arts community mourned losing the most talented of a generation in the AIDS crisis. I wonder if the church did as well.

Even as The Episcopal Church struggled to find its way in this cultural milieu, a new phenomenon was emerging in our public life: the Moral Majority and the "culture wars." It was as if a new line in the sand had been drawn, and marriage and family was the battleground. In retrospect, they were correct; society was moving rapidly toward the full and unprecedented inclusion of gay and lesbian people.

A Church Comes Out

In 1994 the category of sexual orientation was added to the church canon prohibiting discrimination in admission to the process of selection for ordination. That canon was sorely tested in 1996, when the Rt. Rev. **Walter Righter**, retired bishop of Iowa, was charged with heresy for ordaining an out gay man, Barry Stopfel, as a deacon in 1990.

The eventual ruling was carefully nuanced. It stated that a 1979 resolution of General Convention—which included the language "We believe it is not appropriate for this Church to ordain a practicing homosexual or any person who is engaged in heterosexual relations outside of marriage"—was only recommendatory, not mandatory. In other words, it did not say, "This church shall not ordain . . . " This language is as close as we came as a church to prohibiting the ordination of a gay or lesbian person. As a result you will not find a resolution permitting the ordination of a gay or lesbian person, but you will find language prohibiting discrimination on the basis of sexual orientation.

The Anglican Communion responded with approbation. The 1998 **Lambeth Conference**, the every-ten-years meeting of bishops of the Anglican Communion, stated that homosexuality is "incompatible with Scripture," but also committed to "listening to the experience of homosexuals."

For many churches the report from Lambeth, which seemed to pit the Global South against The Episcopal Church and the

Anglican Church of Canada, contradicted their experiences of long-held relationships with parish partners around the globe. Some initiated new partnerships with parishes and LGBT advocates in parts of the communion whose bishops had been most outspoken at Lambeth.

Change Ripples through the Communion

The church pushed the needle even further in 2003, when The Rev. Canon **Gene Robinson** was elected bishop coadjutor of the Diocese of New Hampshire. His election was confirmed later that summer at General Convention, and Robinson became the first openly gay person elected bishop in the Anglican Communion.

Robinson's election caused an even greater uproar in the church. For some it was the culmination of a lifetime of activism for full equality. Others felt compelled to join an exodus from The Episcopal Church, including efforts to separate church property from the diocese, in violation of the canons of the church. Some dioceses sought to leave The Episcopal Church as a whole, aligning with Anglican churches in the Global South. A decade of negotiation, legal battles, and untold expense was to follow.

In October 2004, a commission appointed by Archbishop of Canterbury Rowan Williams issued the **Windsor Report**. The statement reprimanded The Episcopal Church for Gene Robinson's election, and the Anglican Church of Canada for allowing the blessing of same-sex unions in the Diocese of New Westminster. It asked The Episcopal Church for an explanation, which the church provided in *To Set Our Hope on Christ*.

In 2006, the General Convention of The Episcopal Church passed a resolution urging dioceses not to elect partnered gay bishops, and the following year the House of Bishops confirmed that decision. Both decisions were made under considerable pressure from the Archbishop of Canterbury and designed to prevent threatened schism. This decision generated three years of intensive activism, education, and organizing by Episcopalians.

The next General Convention, in 2009, changed course and voted to end the moratorium on electing gay bishops. The Rev. Canon **Mary Glasspool** was elected suffragan bishop of Los Angeles in 2010, making her the second out gay bishop in The Episcopal Church.

In this same time period, from the 1990s into the first decade of the century, an interesting parallel phenomenon was emerging around the Anglican Communion. The churches of the Global South, many of them recently independent churches in nations newly liberated from the British Empire, were flourishing as evangelical Anglican churches. The culture wars made their way around the globe, carried by American evangelicals who were eager to create allies in developing nations.

The Episcopal Church found itself utterly enmeshed and somewhat perplexed by these cultural realities. While we had spent forty years discerning the place of gay and lesbian members within our church, we were ill prepared to explain ourselves in the rest of the Anglican Communion. Because of the American-led wars in Iraq and Afghanistan, the United States had become isolated from the international community. In fact, opponents accused The Episcopal Church of engaging in a "preemptive strike" and "colonial enterprise" through our approval of LGBT inclusion.

Marriage for All

In the first decade of the twenty-first century, **marriage equality** was the primary site of the struggle for equality in the church.

It is worth noting that the Bible says very little about marriage that most of us would wish for our families or ourselves. For the apostle Paul, marriage is described in 1 Corinthians 7 as a sometimes necessary evil. For Jesus, it is only mentioned in Matthew 19, in the context of the contract for divorce. In the Hebrew

Scriptures, the understanding of marriage is very different from any concept that we would hold to today.

Meanwhile, throughout the Anglican Church, liturgies to bless same-sex couples have been in use for decades. In the early years, marriage equality, domestic partnership, and even civil unions were unimaginable, so these liturgies were simply a private, pastoral opportunity for family and friends to gather in support.

In 1999 California and Vermont became the first states to recognize domestic partnerships/civil unions and allow same-sex partners the state privileges of marriage. A decade later, in 2009, the General Convention of The Episcopal Church permitted "generous pastoral response" in dioceses where civil jurisdictions permitted same-gender marriage, civil unions, or domestic partnerships. The church also authorized the study and preparation of rites for the blessing of same-gender relationships.

The Episcopal Church approved "**I Will Bless You and You Will Be a Blessing**," a liturgy for same-sex blessing, in 2012. The liturgy is prefaced by an explanation of the vocation, structures, and blessings of mutual relationships for all genders. The church took another step in 2015 by approving a change in the marriage canon to recognize marriage equality.

Looking ahead, marriage equality is being contested around the world, and it is becoming easier to imagine a time when the church will reflect the growing acceptance in civil society of same-sex marriage. A 2010 Pew Report found that support for same-sex marriage was largely a generational issue. In 2015, 55 percent of Americans supported same-sex marriage. Among Americans born after 1980, 70 percent support same-sex marriage.

• • •

Although The Episcopal Church and the United States government have approved marriage equality, equality is not yet a lived reality throughout the land. Bishops and priests may decline to marry a same-sex couple for no reason other than that they are a same-sex couple. In 2016 states were still passing legislation to allow religious groups to discriminate against LGBT people and their families in defiance of federal equality laws.

The church has taken long strides since those initial moves in 1976. Inevitably, new frontiers will open as we seek to be faithful in the changing cultural landscapes where God calls us to live out the gospel of love.

TO PONDER

1. Have you noticed changing attitudes toward homosexuality in your circle of family and friends? What is changing? Why?

2. Have you noticed changing attitudes toward marriage in your circle of family and friends? What is changing? Why?

3. In 1985, Presiding Bishop Edmund Browning said, "This church of ours is open to all—there will be no outcasts." Is this a goal worth pursuing? How would you measure our progress?

Chapter 7

Gender Fluidity

Gender can seem like such a natural and obvious part of the human experience that it can be hard for some to imagine we need to discuss it. And yet, in 2016 the freedom to claim one's own gender identity is a front-line issue in our cultural and political life. There is no grasping justice or contemporary society without talking about gender identity.

Gender Defined

Gender is the expression of maleness or femaleness that we humans do in varying degrees depending upon the norms for the cultures we live within. In Western cultures gender is usually understood as binary; one is either a woman or a man. In some cultures there are three genders, and in some, gender is understood as on a continuum.

A person whose gender expression correlates with their sex at birth, is called *cis*-**gender** (from the Latin meaning "on the side of"). A person whose gender expression diverges from their visible anatomy, and who might or might not choose to alter their body, is *trans*-gender (from the Latin meaning "across from, or on the other side of").

From time immemorial, we have the stories of people whose gender expression is different from their visible sexual organs. Since the beginning some humans have been born with ambiguous genitalia or the sexual organs of both sexes. Many cultures have historically acknowledged and accepted a third gender, and increasingly in the West the voices of trans women and men are being honored. How have we reckoned with those ambiguities as Christians and as a church?

The Bible and Trans Identity

In the Genesis 1 story of creation, God created a human being, male and female—"ha-adam," which translates as "of earth" or "an earth creature." Ha-adam is often misinterpreted as the proper name "Adam."

Phyllis Trible and other noted Hebrew Bible scholars remind us that in Genesis 2, the first human is again called ha-adam, a Hebrew word, not a proper name. Until the man and the woman are pulled apart from the creature, until the creature is separated into two, it is one, a bi-gendered creature.

In the Bible the other term laden with implications for gender identity is *eunuch*. A eunuch is defined as someone who has either altered his or her sexual organs or takes on a role that is gender transgressive. In Deuteronomy 23:1–3, eunuchs were explicitly denied access to temple worship because they were blemished. Yet Jesus, when asked about marriage, refers to eunuchs:

> For there are eunuchs who have been so from birth, and there are eunuchs who have been made eunuchs by others, and there are eunuchs who have made themselves eunuchs for the sake of the kingdom of heaven. Let anyone accept this who can. (Matthew 19:12)

In Acts 8, Philip is directed by an angel of God to approach and discuss Scripture with an Ethiopian eunuch. Eventually, the eunuch asks, "What would keep me from being baptized?" Philip's legitimate response to the eunuch could have been, "Well, your gender expression!" Everything about the eunuch kept him from entering the temple according to the law, but the passage ends with Phillip baptizing the eunuch, making him one of the first gentiles to follow Jesus. Phillip is actually taken and removed from the scene by divine intervention, so that his encounter with the eunuch is not by chance, but a divine decision.

It is worth noting that the passage Philip interprets with the Ethiopian eunuch is Isaiah 53. Just a few chapters later, we have a direct reference to the place of eunuchs in the reign of God:

> Do not let the foreigner joined to the Lord say,
> "The Lord will surely separate me from his people";
> and do not let the eunuch say,
> "I am just a dry tree."

> For thus says the Lord:
> To the eunuchs who keep my sabbaths,
> who choose the things that please me
> and hold fast my covenant,
> I will give, in my house and within my walls,
> a monument and a name
> better than sons and daughters;
> I will give them an everlasting name
> that shall not be cut off. (Isaiah 56:3–8)

What could all this mean for the place of gender-nonconforming and gender-fluid people in the church? Is this a special focus for those who might feel excluded? Perhaps a special focus to show the church something essential about the dream of God for humanity?

The Missionary Church and Gender Identity

Transgender as a gender identity is perceived differently throughout the Anglican Communion, in some places in defiance of colonial practices, in some places deeply informed by the teaching of missionaries about gender expression and sexuality.

Missionary writings from the colonial era are striking for the ease with which they apply the standards of their sending communities to the new contexts where they serve. In many cases, especially in places where there was a more flexible cultural understanding of gender, the consequences were quite harmful. Because of the timing of the most significant missionary movements, these ambassadors of the faith were influenced by a particularly rigid Victorian social norm in the emerging working class and middle class appearing in European and American cities.

A number of factors moved us toward the narrow understanding of gender we have today. The increase in hospital births and urban and suburban living created a visibility to gender that would have been lived out quite differently in rural communities when births were usually at home. Doctors at times assigned gender at birth by surgery to make babies appear "normal"; some of those affected by these surgeries were closely followed, and their long-term suffering is well documented.

The centering of gender identity as a primary site of social control by Christian nations might seem inevitable now, but it has not always been the case. It could have been decided in many ways, but we ended up with one way to be a family, and our biology determined what roles men and women play in that family.

Putting the "T" into LGBT

Through decades of persistence, in the twenty-first century we find a visible movement to make discrimination based on gender expression illegal. Today, we see transgender people in the media. Many communities celebrate children who claim their trans identity early in life, and we support families that love and encourage their children publicly. The Episcopal group dedicated to trans advocacy is **Trans Episcopal**; learn more about them at http://blog.transepiscopal.com.

There is still much work to do for transgender inclusion in the church and in society. For instance, we are made aware through social media of the almost daily murder of transgender people throughout the United States.

We are at a turning point in the United States and in The Episcopal Church, one that has been a long time coming. In 2009 the 76th General Convention supported federal laws that prohibit employment discrimination because of sexual orientation or gender identity. The next General Convention pushed further still and amended the canons to include gender identity and expression among protected areas for those seeking rights, status, and equal access in the church.

• • •

Some people have been surprised by the speed with which the church has officially received transgender members and leaders. In fact, we have always been more than simply male and female, although culture has tried hard to create a clean binary. Gender identity, whether you understand yourself as male, female, or in another way, is a social construct.

There are many ways to live on this earth, and we are discerning in this time what it means to best love people who experience their gender differently from what society expects. In the church, sensitivity to gender identity includes care in using pronouns and taking care with assumptions about gender based on physical appearance. We honor each other's words and take them into our own hearts. We promise in our Baptismal Covenant to "respect the dignity of every human being."

Self-definition is primary to dignity, and we are blessed as Episcopalians that our prayers guide us as we seek to see Christ in others.

TO PONDER

1. Have you ever been asked to claim your preferred gender pronoun? How would you answer? How does this question make you feel?

2. Scholars like Phyllis Trible suggest that in Genesis, the original human being was both male and female. What do you think of this theory?

3. What issues of gender justice are you aware of in your church or community?

Interlude

What Is "Intersectionality"?

Intersectionality is a term used in legal scholarship, critical theory, and activism, and it describes the curious moment when a person falls "between the cracks" because they have multiple markers of identity, but the culture cannot recognize this multiplicity.

Professor Kimberle Crenshaw, who wrote about a case against General Motors on behalf of black women in 1976, coined the term. In that case the court ruled that the plaintiffs could file a case as black people or as women, but not as both, even though it was the intersection of the two that caused the kinds of discrimination they were facing. Other useful terms to describe this phenomenon are interlocking or simultaneous oppressions or double or triple jeopardy. Whatever the language, in social movements and in our work to be reconciled to one another, intersectionality gives us a way to claim our multiple identities, understand what is happening when we are forced or force others to choose to speak from only one identity at a time, and the complementary or conflicting perspectives that can come with multiple identities.

The most famous example of intersectionality is from Sojourner Truth, the black liberation leader whose "Ain't I a Woman" speech to the 1851 Women's Convention in Akron, Ohio, illustrates the challenge of living between worlds:

> That man over there says that women need to be helped into carriages and lifted over ditches, and to have the best place everywhere. Nobody ever helps me into carriages, or over mud-puddles, or gives me any best place! And ain't I a woman? Look at me! Look at my arm! I could have ploughed and planted, and gathered into barns, and no man could head me! And ain't I a woman? I could work as much and eat as much as a man—when I could get it—and bear the lash as well! And ain't I a woman? I have borne thirteen children, and seen them most all sold off to slavery, and when I cried out with my mother's grief, none but Jesus heard me! And ain't I a woman?

Naming the overlapping nature and complexity of identity is important in social movements, so that the wholeness of each individual is truly considered in the work of liberation. There are many descriptors of the human experience that apply: race, ethnicity, class, education, gender identity, sexual orientation, physical ability, and physical and mental illness. Identities can be visible or invisible, and even though they are societal categories, these categories frame our experience in the world.

The Stonewall Riots in 1969 are described as a turning point in the Gay Liberation Movement. When I imagine that movement in Manhattan, I imagine young, middle-class, white men fighting to be seen as just like everyone else. In fact, poor, transgender women of color led the Stonewall riots. Those identity distinctions matter today, as well. In 2016, a transgender woman of color is killed every twenty-nine hours in the United States.

Intersectionality in and of itself does not mean that we, because of an awareness of our multiple identities, are able to understand all or even more experiences. It does mean we have the capacity to see multiple categories and begin to create the intellectual and emotional space to recognize and honor the complexity of the lives around us.

TO PONDER

1. Perform a quick self-check: how does the idea of intersectionality make you feel: understood, confused, frustrated?

2. In the General Motors case, the ruling stated that the black women who had brought the case could not benefit doubly from antidiscrimination ordinances and had to choose one, black or woman. Have you ever had to choose an identity?

3. Intersectionality asks each of us to name our intersecting identities. Can you think of a situation in which your multiple identities inform or enrich your experience in unexpected ways?

Chapter 8

Jesus and the 99 Percent

After loving God and neighbor—or perhaps illustrative of loving God and neighbor—are the commands to be makers of a just society by participating in, acting as if, God's justice could be true now. From Exodus to Proverbs and through the Gospels, treating those who are economically vulnerable with mercy is a mark of loving God. We see it in passages like this:

> You shall not oppress a hired servant who is poor and needy, whether he is one of your countrymen or one of your aliens who is in your land in your towns. You shall give him his wages on his day before the sun sets, for he is poor and sets his heart on it; so that he will not cry against you to the LORD and it become sin in you. (Deuteronomy 24:14–15)

In the early Christian community the disciples took this message seriously. Jesus's followers gathered in communities within which resources were pooled and shared to the benefit of the least. "All who believed were together and had all things in common; they would sell their possessions and goods and distribute the proceeds to all, as any had need" (Acts 2:44–45).

The Episcopal Church today lives in the shadow of this witness. The gift and burden of our legacy as a church includes a responsibility to be a part of the rebuilding of a just society.

Poverty Today

In the United States alone, 45 million people live in poverty. This figure includes 16 million children, or one in five. The social safety net, for those who lose their jobs or fall on hard times, is shredded in most of this country, and the basics of life are prohibitively expensive for many: a good job, education, health care, a home, and even nutritious food. To share what little we have might seem absurd.

As a church, and as a society, the call of God to us is to share the abundance of creation so that all may live with dignity. When we are talking about millions of people, we need government policy to support the most vulnerable, an increase in the minimum wage, food support, access to health care, good public schools, and decent, affordable housing.

In other parts of The Episcopal Church—like Haiti, the Dominican Republic, or Ecuador—the choice to lift the poor out of poverty is more difficult to resource, particularly in countries where foreign parties like the United States influence local leadership, and yet, we find the church in those places actively serving the most vulnerable as a matter of course. Poverty is assumed to be a problem that concerns the church. That is not necessarily the case in the United States. In a country as wealthy as the United States, choosing these priorities is a matter of will, not resource.

Note the Census Bureau's annual poverty report. Included within the report is how much money it would take, through programs we already have in place, to lift every family at least to the poverty line. In 2012 it was $175.3 billion, or about 1 percent of gross domestic product. For perspective, that is one quarter of military spending that year.

The eradication of poverty in the United States is possible. We must then ask ourselves why we choose to abandon one in five of our children and their families.

Theologically, we are not a tradition that asks the suffering to wait for their reward in the next life. Because of the Incarnation, or God's choice to come and dwell among us, Episcopalians see and honor the humanity of those among us who struggle to sustain themselves, and that means we must all work to build a society in which poor people can attain a decent way of life.

Domestic Poverty Fellow Sarah Monroe describes a program to support movements to end poverty, led by people experiencing poverty:

> The purpose is not only to treat the symptoms of hunger and lack of resources but to support leadership in poor communities with the people on the street, people experiencing poverty, to develop a movement really to end poverty in this county and to develop a model to do it elsewhere. That's a big dream, but it's one worth having.[1]

In The Episcopal Church, many of our congregations respond with feeding programs and other efforts to help the needy in our communities. The statistics above point to the need for a more permanent and system-wide solution. Our acts of charity are important, but advocacy with the poor among us can change lives for generations.

Church of the Elite

According to the Pew Research Center on Religion in Public Life in 2014, 36 percent of Episcopalians make more than $100,000 a year, and 68 percent make more than $50,000. Among American Christians, Episcopalians have the highest proportion of high

---

1. Mary Frances Schjonberg, "Domestic Poverty Fellows Work to Alleviate Suffering, Teach Church" (Episcopal Café, February 26, 2015).

incomes and are the most highly educated. Only about 25 percent of Americans make more than $50,000 a year, and 8 percent of Americans make more than $100,000 a year.

The statistical case goes further. Thirty-one percent of Episcopalians have a bachelor's degree, 25 percent have graduate degrees, and 84 percent have graduated high school. Compare that to the 22 percent of American adults who have graduated with a bachelor's degree and about 9 percent who have earned a graduate degree.

Although many Episcopalians struggle to stay afloat, The Episcopal Church is overall a church of the elite, even among other mainline Protestants.

As economic disparity once more becomes a marker of U.S. society, and the memory of a time when those disparities were diminishing because of government policies and investment in the infrastructure of this nation is fresh, we have to reimagine what a Christian role in creating a just society might be.

As Episcopalians, we count among us presidents and other civic leaders who have addressed economic inequality in diverse ways as Republicans and Democrats, including presidents Franklin Roosevelt and George H. W. Bush. These leaders disagreed about approach, and whether the government could do the most good for the most people, or if incentivizing the private sector to provide charity is the most effective way to deal compassionately with economic disparity, but they placed the problem of poverty on the table as one we had an obligation to address.

We are challenged in every generation to discern how to best align our resources with our values. In some generations, selling our properties and spending endowments to fund programs in the community was a high priority. In other times, doing all we can to maintain a vital presence in under-resourced communities is the favored strategy.

There are many approaches, but a commitment to an equitable distribution of resources is fundamental to a Christian worldview.

Episcopalians are part of a tradition with significant power and influence that exercises that power in the world, so addressing poverty at its roots and developing institutions that support the well-being of the most disenfranchised is our work.

Navigating and Occupying Wall Street

Episcopalians participate in the economy at all levels. Some investors believe we make as much money as we can in the stock market, to support the most mission we can. Others argue that the corporations we support through investment are also a site of action and moral engagement. We should support ethical corporations and work for more just corporate practices. Still others would argue that our wealth is our primary tool to effect social change through shareholder activism and investments in under-resourced communities.

Occupy Wall Street, which began in 2011, has transformed how Americans talk about wealth, jobs, housing, and employment. Occupy named the 1 percent, the people who control the economy for their benefit or to the detriment of the 99 percent, almost all of us in the United States. Occupy's success was creating a sense of solidarity among people across income and education levels, who united around the experience of an economic system that is an insecure and terrifying place for 99 percent of the people.

Occupy effectively educated the American public about the abuses of the banking industry and the government's collusion in supporting their corruption. In the United States today foreclosure and eviction rates are horrifying. If holding a mortgage on a home was the first step to financial security and the American dream, that dream has become a nightmare for many Americans. Occupy took a complex message of a system designed to make profit by selling failing mortgages and other products utterly removed from the real human lives entangled in the machinations of the market, and revealed the human cost.

A Just Future

The challenge to The Episcopal Church in this generation is to rebuild communities. In the early twentieth century the church established medical care, education, and nutrition in rapidly industrializing areas. We are in a similar time in the United States and in all of the countries where our church is present. The infrastructure that created opportunity for working Americans has been dismantled since the 1980s. Homelessness, lack of clean water, failing schools, and limited access to health care have once again become norms, not aberrations. In 2015 the top 20 percent of U.S. households owned more than 84 percent of the wealth, and the bottom 40 percent controlled just 0.3 percent. Most Americans expect there to be some disparity in wealth, but not this much.

The church is the front line for help for some of the most desperate in our communities through direct service like food programs and via creative ventures like credit unions that make loans in communities that large banks refuse to support. We are also bearers of another vision for society, one in which all are cared for and there is enough for the flourishing of all.

TO PONDER

1. Are you surprised at the evidence of The Episcopal Church's overall wealth and education? How does this match your own understanding of the church?

2. Many Christians participate in the stock market. What makes an investment ethical for a Christian?

3. Much of the historic infrastructure to address poverty in the United States no longer exists. How, if at all, do you believe the church should respond?

Chapter 9

War and Peace

As Christians we follow Jesus, who could fairly be described as a resister to the Roman Empire. He taught and proclaimed an alternative kingdom in ways so provocative that the Empire put him to death.

Perhaps as a result, from the beginning of the church, followers of Jesus have deplored war and state-sponsored violence, naming them unequivocally evil. Church father Tertullian once observed, "The Lord in disarming Peter henceforth disarms every soldier."

Today some might argue that war is a necessary evil, but as Christians we recognize that the destruction of the bodies of the young and usually poor with machines designed for mutilation and destruction is not a reasonable approach to solving political conflict. That may be why the teachings of the church—Roman Catholic, Orthodox, Anglican, and many Protestants—are strikingly unified in their opposition to war. That theological clarity is not reflected in our public life.

Just War Theory

As the Christian movement evolved from a small, voluntary gathering of people who followed the teachings of Jesus through the early disciples into the religion of first the Roman Empire, and then every subsequent European empire, leaders and theologians like Augustine began to discern the terms of a Christian way to be at war.

In the thirteenth century, Thomas Aquinas further refined Augustine's thinking to set out what is known classically as **Just War Theory**. The two major components are the following:

- *Jus Ad Bellem* or **just reasons to go to war**. These include self-defense, if no other means are available but war. All diplomacy must be exhausted. The intention of war should be justice as understood in sparing human life and increasing access to human rights. The stated outcome should be truly possible and significant enough to justify going to war.

- *Jus In Bello* or **just conduct of war**. For instance, it is fundamentally unjust to attack civilians. Violence must be proportional to the outcome. Soldiers are responsible for their actions. Attacks must have legitimate military objectives. Prisoners of war have basic human rights and dignity; and finally, combatants must not use methods that are evil, like mass rape, or whose effects are disproportionate, like blanket bombings, chemical, biological, or nuclear warfare.

For most traditions, both *Jus Ad Bellem* and *Jus In Bello* are to be exercised with marked compassion for those who will lose their lives in the acts of war. In the end, some argue that the standards are so close to impossible to meet, that the expectation remains that there should rarely if ever be war.

The contemporary American approach to Just War is most famously stated by **Reinhold Neibuhr**, who wrote in the shadow of World War II, after the discovery and liberation of the Nazi concentration camps. Neibuhr claimed that the modern Christian had to deal with political complexity, since the church lives in history and must accept that reality.

Love may qualify the social struggle of history but it will never abolish it, and those who make the attempt to bring society under the dominion of perfect love will die on the cross. And those who behold the cross are quite right in seeing it as a revelation of the divine, of what man ought to be but cannot be, at least not so long as he is enmeshed in the processes of history.[1]

Neibuhr trusted in the power of God, but he rejected the idea that there was any way to be pure or to have completely clean hands with respect to violence. War, for him, was sad but inevitable.

The Age of Fear

In this age of **terrorism**—that is, criminal attack by non-state actors—many powerful nations have resorted to war as a tool to occupy other nations to attempt to eradicate the groups that sponsor terrorism. This policy has often failed or even backfired, strengthening the very terrorist movements it sought to weaken, and it meets none of the criteria of a "just war." And yet, war of this kind has swept the globe for most of the twenty-first century. According to the **Global Peace Index**, in 2014, 151 of the 162 nations in the world were at war. Only eleven countries on the planet enjoy peace.

Why is war so pervasive today? Episcopal ethicist Scott Bader-Saye says it is not that the conditions are different today, rather it comes down to fear:

One reason we are a more fearful culture today, despite the fact that the dangers are not objectively greater than in the past, is because some people have incentives and means to heighten, manipulate, and exploit our fears. Fear is a strong motivator, and so those who

---

1. Reinhold Neibuhr, *Moral Man and Immoral Society* (Louisville, KY: Westminster John Knox, 1932), 417.

want and need to motivate others—politicians, advertisers, media executives, advocacy groups, even the church—turn to fear to bolster their message. I call this the "fear for profit" syndrome, and it is rampant. We have become preoccupied with unlikely dangers that take on the status of imminent threats.[2]

Today, the danger is especially marked because the threat is defined as a religious enemy. Christians and Muslims often work intentionally to cooperate for peace and healing, but we find ourselves trapped in the narrative rooted in the long histories of the Crusades and the colonial periods. It can feel as though we are in the midst of a drama we don't understand.

Churches Waging Peace

Many Christian communities outright reject acts of state violence. They are opposed to war under any circumstances. Among Protestants some denominations or sects even take the name "Peace Churches" (for example the Quakers and Mennonites). For the rest of us there are historic, committed factions within our churches who resist state-sponsored violence by refusing to pay taxes that support the military, rejecting conscription into the military, and working actively to create peace through nonviolent methods.

Through the **Episcopal Peace Fellowship**, Episcopalians organize to resist the culture of fear and violence by developing the courage to bear witness to love. Founded as the Episcopal Pacifist Fellowship after World War I, the Episcopal Peace Fellowship is a voluntary, membership organization of Episcopal lay people and clergy who work for peace. Its mission is promoting cultures of peace and nonviolence, and it moves legislation

---

2. Scott Bader-Saye, *Following Jesus in a Culture of Fear* (Grand Rapids, MI: Brazos Press, 1997), 16.

through the General Convention to keep The Episcopal Church true to the Christian values of peacemaking and reconciliation.

Speaking to the House of Bishops in 1917, EPF founder Paul Jones, bishop of Utah, declared:

> We all feel that war is wrong, evil, and undesirable. Many even feel that war is unchristian but unavoidable, as the world is now constituted, and that the present situation forces us to use it. Some contend that this is a righteous war (World War I), and that we must all fight the devil with fire, even at the danger of being scorched, or all the ideals which we hold dear will go by the board, and therefore we are solemnly, sadly, and earnestly taking that way.
>
> In spite of my respect for the integrity of those who feel bound to take that course, and in spite of the knowledge that I am occupying an unpopular and decidedly minority point of view, I have been led to feel that war is entirely incompatible with the Christian profession.[3]

These words may sound idealistic, but the church is fundamentally idealistic. We believe that Christ through his death, resurrection, and ascension defeats the destructive powers of this world, which might be most clearly represented in war.

All of this is not to avoid a simple fact: Episcopalians hold a wide variety of views on the subject of war. The Episcopal Church has a suffragan bishop for the Armed Forces chaplaincy, and we have many military chaplains. Many Episcopalians serve in the military. Today, when war seems to be the inevitable way of the world, we are challenged by our tradition to discern in our time how to honor the dignity of every human being.

---

3. Don S. Armentrout and Robert Boak Slocum, eds., *Documents of Witness: A History of The Episcopal Church 1782–1985* (New York: Church Hymnal Corporation, 1994), 339.

TO PONDER

1. Christians have struggled with the seeming inevitability of war for millennia. Why might a Christian defend war? Why might a Christian oppose it?

2. Reinhold Niebuhr argues that the world is fallen, and that Christians have to deal in the reality of our time. Are there unchangeable realities in your life that force you to make decisions you might feel are less than true to Christian faith?

Chapter 10

Liturgy and Social Witness

Published in the 1549 Book of Common Prayer, the **Great Litany** is the first liturgical service in English. Most of us use it for the first Sunday in Lent. Few realize it is written for times of distress and conflict, and specifically, times of war.

On Fridays in Lent during the Iraq War, a few of us gathered at the Isaiah Wall in Ralph Bunche Park, across the street from the United Nations building in New York City, to chant the Great Litany in procession—with vestments, incense, processional cross, and torches, of course. The Isaiah Wall proclaims Isaiah 2 in stone: "They shall beat their swords into plowshares. . . . Neither shall they learn war any more."

About forty of us joined in chanting the litany on a success-ful Friday. In the rain and in off weeks, it might have been ten. And, yet, it is those Fridays I remember now most clearly in what was a long season of protest. Bringing the voice of the church to the street, standing as powerless as the rest, in the shadow of the words of Isaiah, and offering the first act of public prayer in English in despair as our prayer for peace, and claiming both the seeming futility and great power of the voice of the church has changed my experience of the Great Litany and of worship.

Praying Shapes Believing

For Episcopalians the liturgy is everything. Seriously. The effort it took to produce and secure use of the 1979 Prayer Book may be unparalleled in our history. It is, of course, the language with which we approach God. It frames how we experience ourselves in relationship to God, and for many of us liturgy has been the space in which our most profound experiences of the sacred have occurred.

There is always a danger of idolatry for Anglicans in one liturgical moment or the other. At our best, liturgy is a lively practice that raises us to participate with God in refashioning the world as God would have it. At our worst, we believe what is most aesthetically pleasing to us should be mandated for all.

F. D. Maurice once preached, "I do not think we are to praise the liturgy but to use it. When we do not want it for our life, we may begin to talk of it as a beautiful composition."[1] If we use our liturgy, we are transformed into closer alignment with how God sees the world.

This can be a terrifying place to be. The unjustness of the world breaks our hearts. It makes sense that some would hold a tense rigidity in liturgy to protect their hearts from the devastation of the truths that are revealed in the practice of prayer. The practice itself forms us into people and communities that can bear much more pain and truth than we would have guessed, and liturgy equips us to act on behalf of God's vision for the world.

The Eucharistic Feast, which is at the center of our liturgy in the current prayer book, is the central act of the historic church. Protestant churches, of which we are part, shifted the emphasis from the table (Eucharist) to the word (reading the Bible and preaching) in response to a cruel and oppressive centralized controlling of the sacraments. The Episcopal Church combines the

---

1. F. D. Maurice, *Sermons on the Prayer Book* (1880), 6.

two. We hold to the centrality of the Eucharist and the necessity of bringing human capacity to the ordering of the body of Christ.

Paul Moore, a trailblazing lover of justice and bishop of New York, wrote often of the connection between Eucharist and social action.

> The place and time where all these ideas and relationships come true is in the Eucharist. Here is the pattern and the power. . . . Here, as Charles Williams would say, is the time and place for an exchange—an exchange of my burden for yours, an exchange of our burdens for the light yoke of Christ, an exchange of sin and penitence for forgiveness. And in the Consecration of the bread and wine is an exchange of our bodies for his body, of the Cross for Resurrection, of captivity for freedom, of death for life, of all else for joy.[2]

One aspect of centering our lives on the Eucharist is that the vision of the reign of God—in which resurrection, freedom, life and joy are supreme—is always before us. Our worship calls us into an awareness of the timeless, mysterious perfection of the reign of God by narrating the great acts of God, all done in prayerful attentiveness to God at work in the world today. In light of these great mysteries, we are emboldened to imagine anew what God's justice looks like in the world around us.

Liturgy and the Social Gospel

In The Episcopal Church the Social Gospel was primarily, although not exclusively, carried through Anglo-Catholic churches in cities. **Anglo-Catholic** in this context refers to a eucharistically centered liturgy with a strong emphasis on the ceremony of the rite, which is said to reflect the prayers and praise always being offered in heaven.

---

2. Paul Moore, *The Church Reclaims the City* (Seabury Press, 1964), 221.

This nineteenth- and early twentieth-century liturgical movement had everything to do with social action. Anglo-Catholics founded Sunday Schools (often the only schools for poor, immigrant kids), feeding programs, health clinics, day cares, and camps. The church later influenced the establishment of New Deal and Great Society programs that attempted to raise an entire nation out of poverty.

The connection between liturgy, the ancient hymns and rites of the church, and social action is a faint but persistent strain in The Episcopal Church. **Jonathan Daniels**, the Episcopal Theological School student martyred during the Civil Rights Movement, was stirred while singing the Magnificat in the same week that Martin Luther King Jr. called the nation to join him in Selma to march to Montgomery. Daniels detailed that conversion experience in this way:

> I had come to Evening Prayer as usual that evening, and as usual I was singing the Magnificat with the special love and reverence I have always felt for Mary's glad song. "He hath showed strength with his arm." As the lovely hymn of the God-bearer continued, I found myself peculiarly alert, suddenly straining toward the decisive, luminous, Spirit-filled "moment" that would, in retrospect, remind me of others—particularly one at Easter three years ago. Then it came. "He hath put down the mighty from their seat, and hath exalted the humble and meek. He hath filled the hungry with good things." I knew then that I must go to Selma. The Virgin's song was to grow more and more dear in the weeks ahead.[3]

This is the power of worship, of liturgy. In our practice of the ritual, the very course of our lives can be changed.

---

3. Jonathan Myrick Daniels, "Biographical Sketches of Memorable Christians of the Past," http://justus.anglican.org/resources/bio/228.html.

• • •

The primary work of the liturgy is among us, the faithful. We approach worship expectantly, eager to touch the hem of Jesus's garment or to eat the bread of life. Public prayer orients us, we who seek to live our days in the depths of our humanity, aligning our wills with God's desires.

Inside a church building or out on the street, liturgy is how we reenact the sacred drama of our relationship to God. That is why liturgy is for us the ultimate act.

TO PONDER

1. How does liturgy influence your understanding of yourself and the world?

2. Bishop Paul Moore makes a case for why the Eucharist is so central for Christian life, especially for social action. Would you agree? Why would the Eucharist be so important?

3. Singing the Magnificat during Evening Prayer, Jonathan Daniels felt a call to join the Civil Rights Movement. Can you recall a time that participating in liturgy changed your experience of the world or stirred you to any sort of action?

Conclusion
To Live "As If"

William Porcher Dubose, Confederate Army chaplain and theologian, made this prescient comment on social issues in the nineteenth century:

> The world is constantly outgrowing and making sinful institutions which, however they are so now, were not so to it in the age or at the stage in which they prevailed. Polygamy was no sin to Abraham. Slavery was no sin in the consciousness or conscience of the New Testament. Feudalism was no sin in its day, but would be so now. Puritanism in forms which were once admirable would now be condemned. The time will come when war will be a sin.[1]

Slavery was no sin to Dubose or to his fellow Confederate soldiers not too long before these words were written, and possibly not to many of his colleagues when he chose to share the sentiment above. We too humbly seek to understand the world around us in faithful discernment.

In the twenty-first century, we Episcopalians have work to do. First, we have to understand sin as an active force in the world around us, one over which we have very limited if any power. From there, we can recognize our desperate need for God. The

---

1. Richard H. Schmidt, *Glorious Companions: Five Centuries of Anglican Spirituality* (Grand Rapids, MI: Wm. B. Eerdmans, 2002), 203.

response of God to sin and death is resurrection and the utterly improbable reign of God's justice.

If we seek to see the beauty of God's reign, we can also live as though it is true today. We commit ourselves to this vision in our baptism, and we participate in a foretaste of the reign of God's love in the Eucharist. From there, we are compelled to take it to the world.

We have many voices in the Episcopal Church to carry us forward. The words of Episcopal theologian **Kelly Brown Douglas** may be the most compelling in this moment:

> We must dare to live proleptically, that is, as if, god's promised future is already. The manner in which we conduct our living should be but a foretaste of god's time. This means that we must live as if every single human being, regardless of their language, their color, their country of origin, their income, their education, deserves food, clothing, shelter, care, because they do. We are to live as if the bigotry, fear, stereotypes, and hateful "isms" that separate us one from another are no more. We are to live as if compassion not condemnation, justice not judgment, and righteousness not self-righteousness are the watchwords of our humanity. We are to live as if the peace of god that is justice has come to earth. Even if these ways of acting are not the ways of our world, we must be daring enough to make them the way of our living.[2]

May it be so.

---

2. Kelly Brown Douglas, "How Is It That God Speaks?", January 21, 2014, www.feminismandreligion.com.

www.ingramcontent.com/pod-product-compliance
Lightning Source LLC
Jackson TN
JSHW081320130125
77033JS00011B/366